SYNONYMS SIGHT WORDS

THESAURUS FOR KIDS
SAME OR DIFFERENT FOR KIDS
CHILDREN'S EDUCATION & REFERENCE BOOKS

BoBo's Little Brainiac Books

educational & informative books for children
(PRE-K / K-12)

All Rights reserved. No part of this book may be reproduced or used in any way or form or by any means whether electronic or mechanical, this means that you cannot record or photocopy any material ideas or tips that are provided in this book

Copyright 2016

PRACTICE TRACING AND WRITING THE WORDS!

end   finish

Rewrite the words.

cry   sob

Rewrite the words.

cold   icy

Rewrite the words.

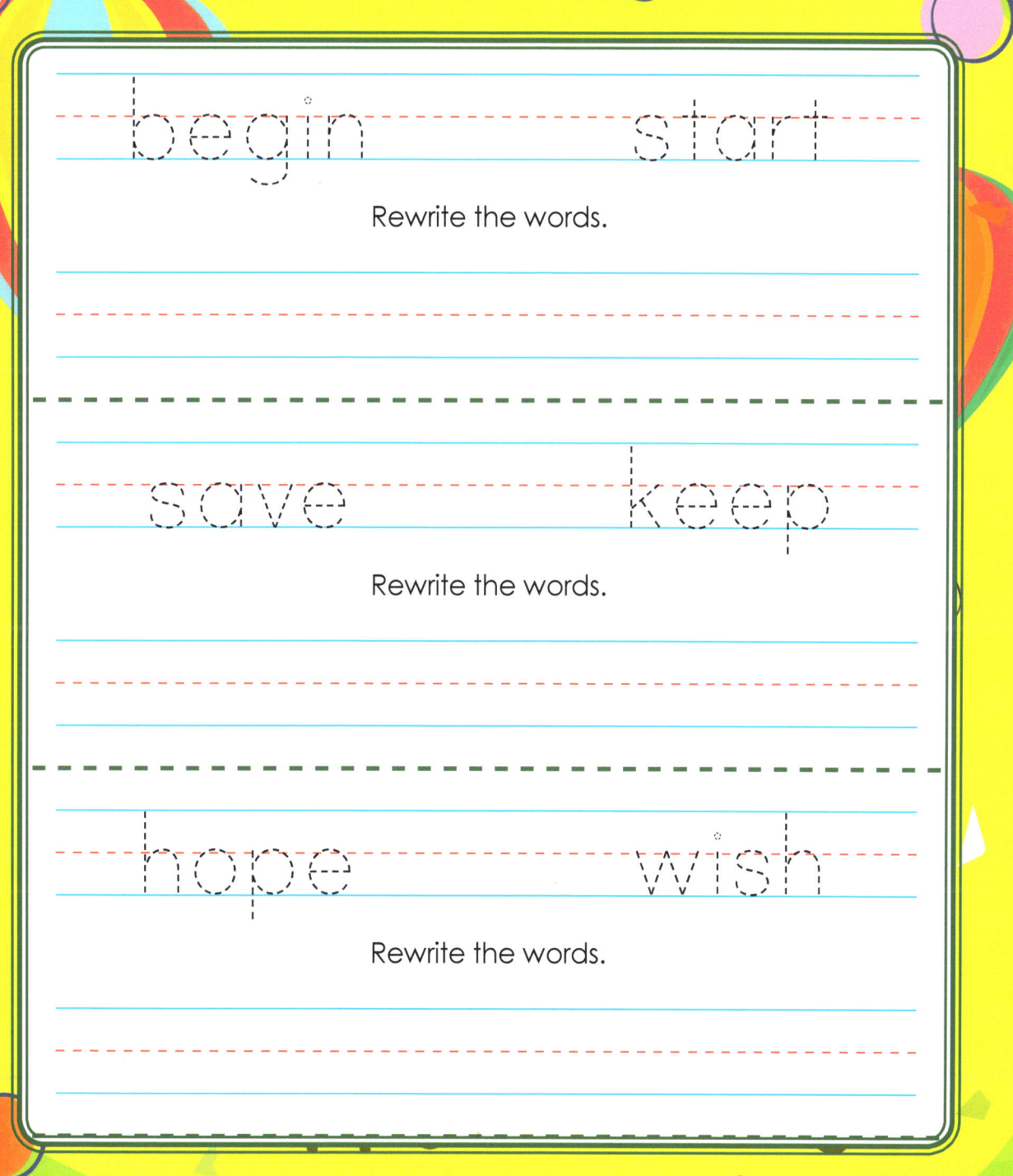

small   little

Rewrite the words.

mother   mom

Rewrite the words.

father   dad

Rewrite the words.

house   home

Rewrite the words.

woman   lady

Rewrite the words.

child   kid

Rewrite the words.

ill   sick

Rewrite the words.

see   look

Rewrite the words.

alike   similar

Rewrite the words.

evil   bad

Rewrite the words.

happy   glad

Rewrite the words.

angry   mad

Rewrite the words.

shout yell

Rewrite the words.

kind nice

Rewrite the words.

rich wealthy

Rewrite the words.

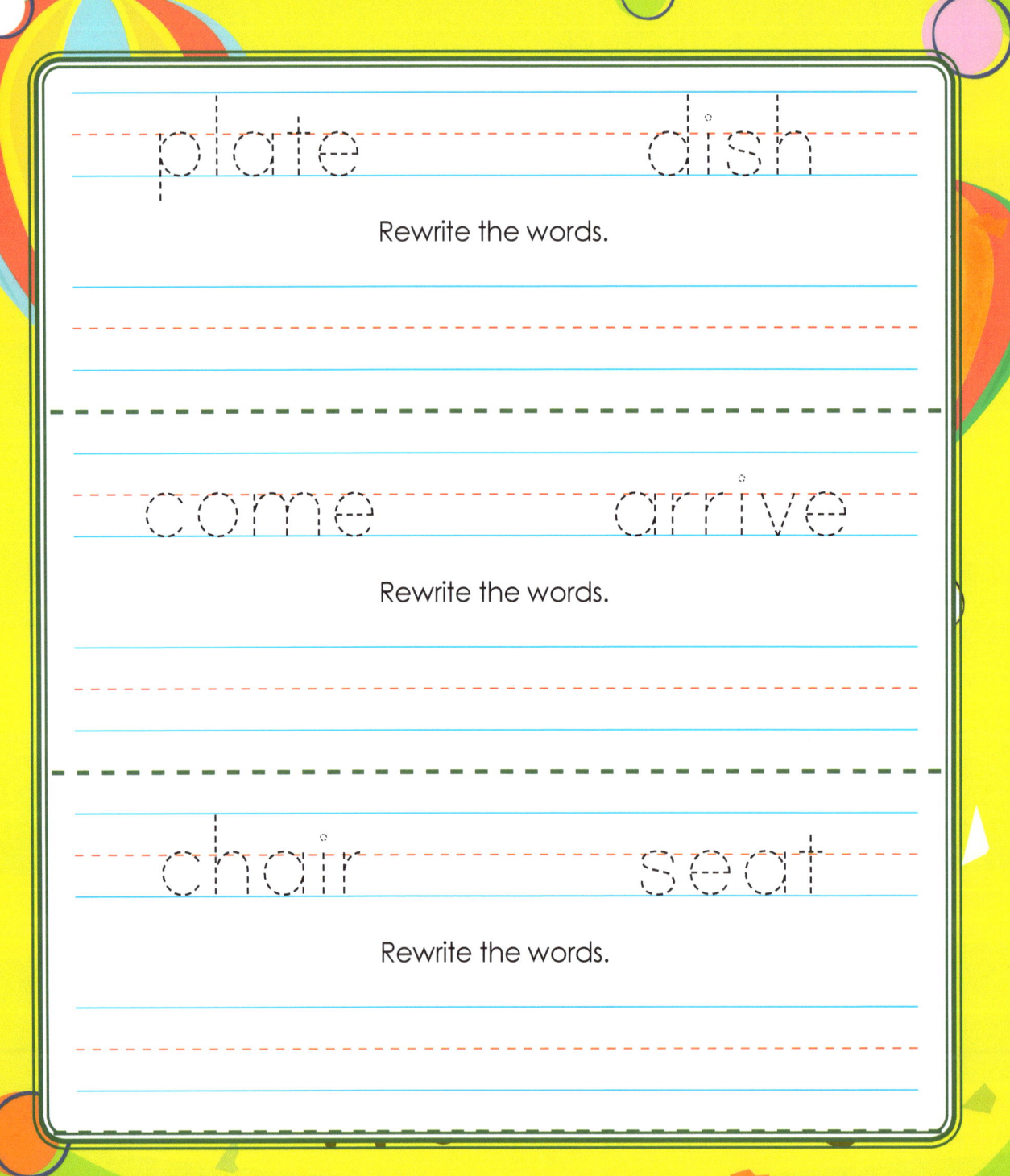

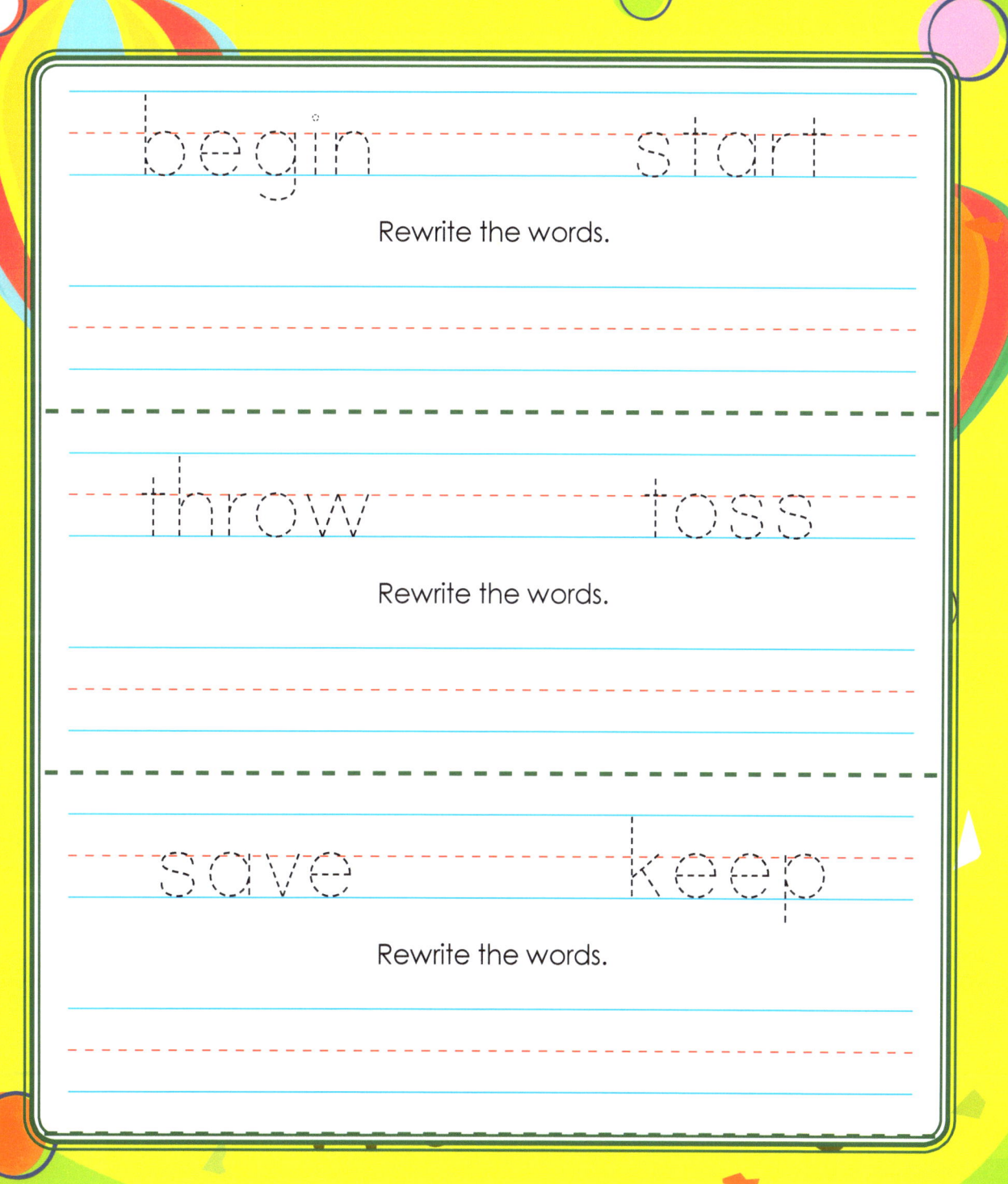

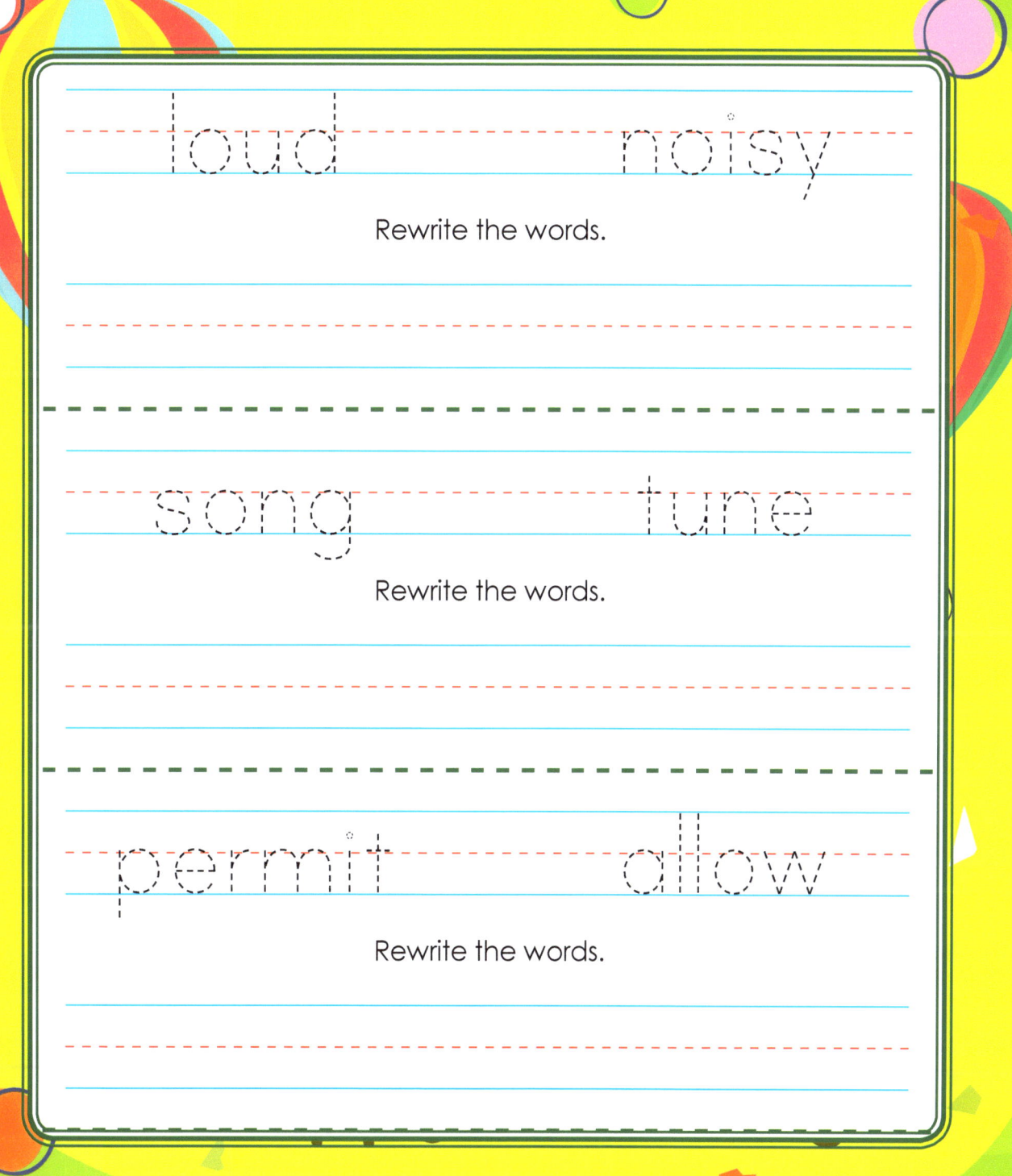

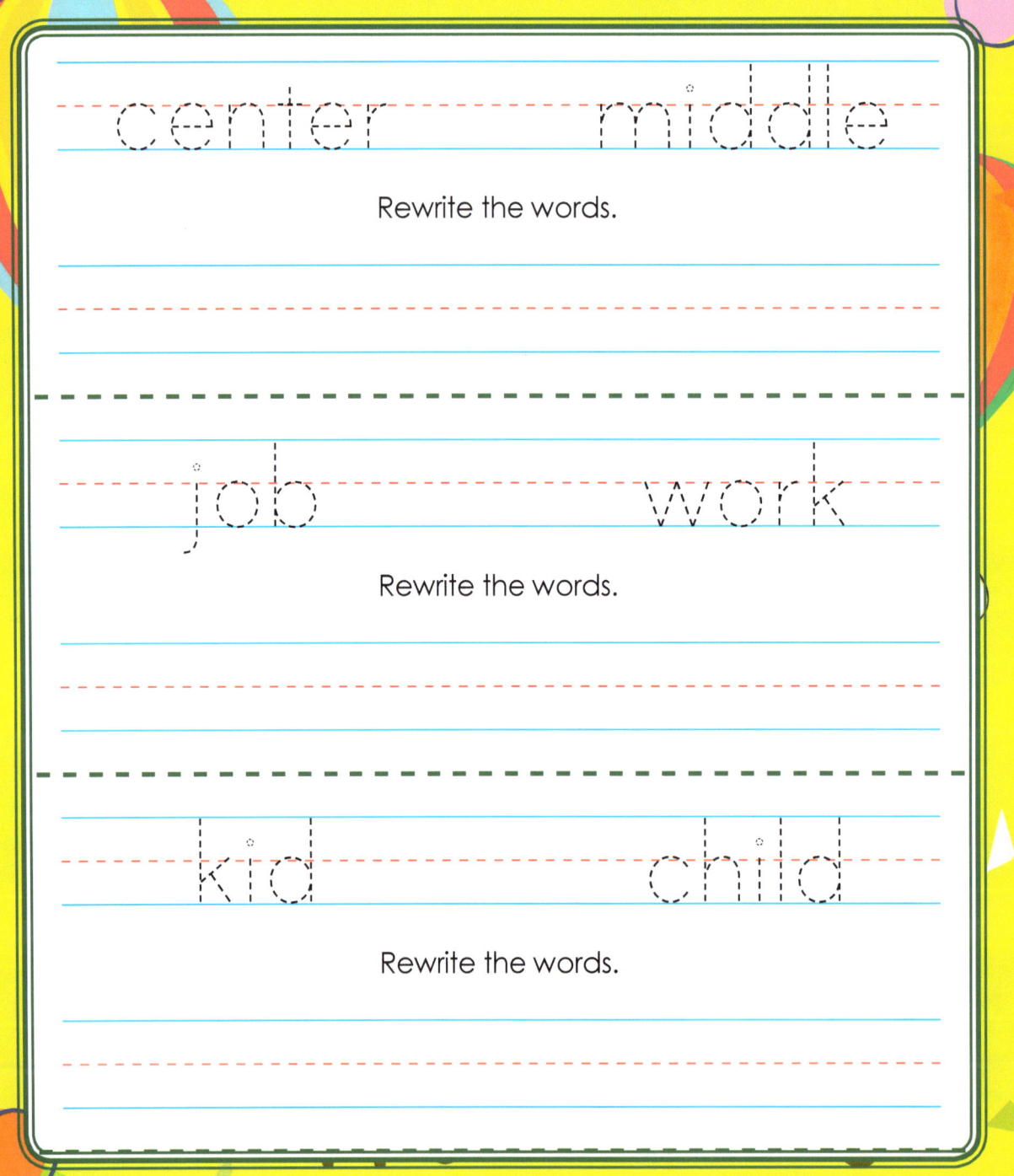

old mature

Rewrite the words.

scared afraid

Rewrite the words.

blank empty

Rewrite the words.

broad	wide

Rewrite the words.

cunning	clever

Rewrite the words.

false	untrue

Rewrite the words.

hard   difficult

Rewrite the words.

high   tall

Rewrite the words.

new   modern

Rewrite the words.

oral   verbal

Rewrite the words.

rare   scarce

Rewrite the words.

ready   alert

Rewrite the words.

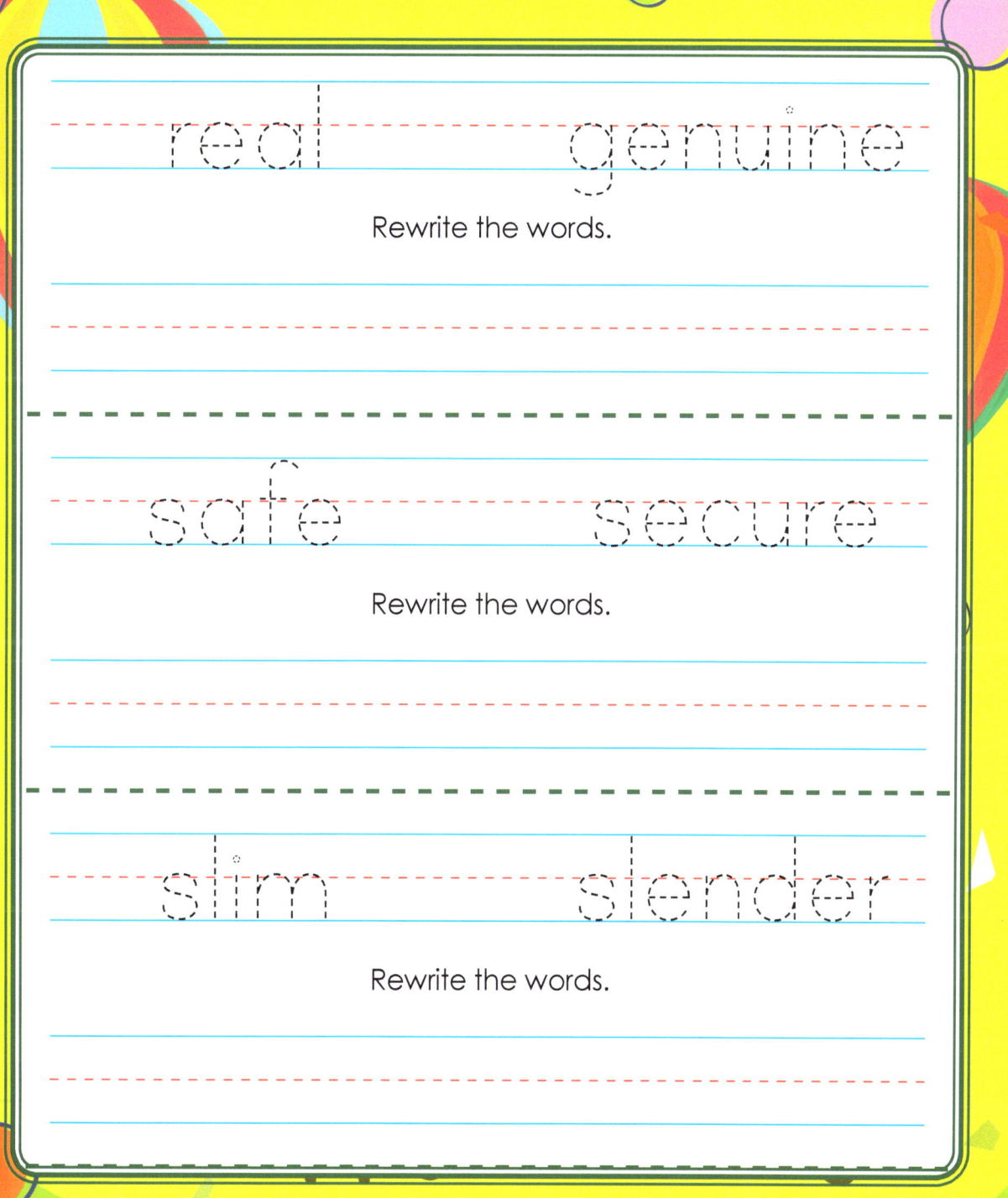

real genuine

Rewrite the words.

safe secure

Rewrite the words.

slim slender

Rewrite the words.

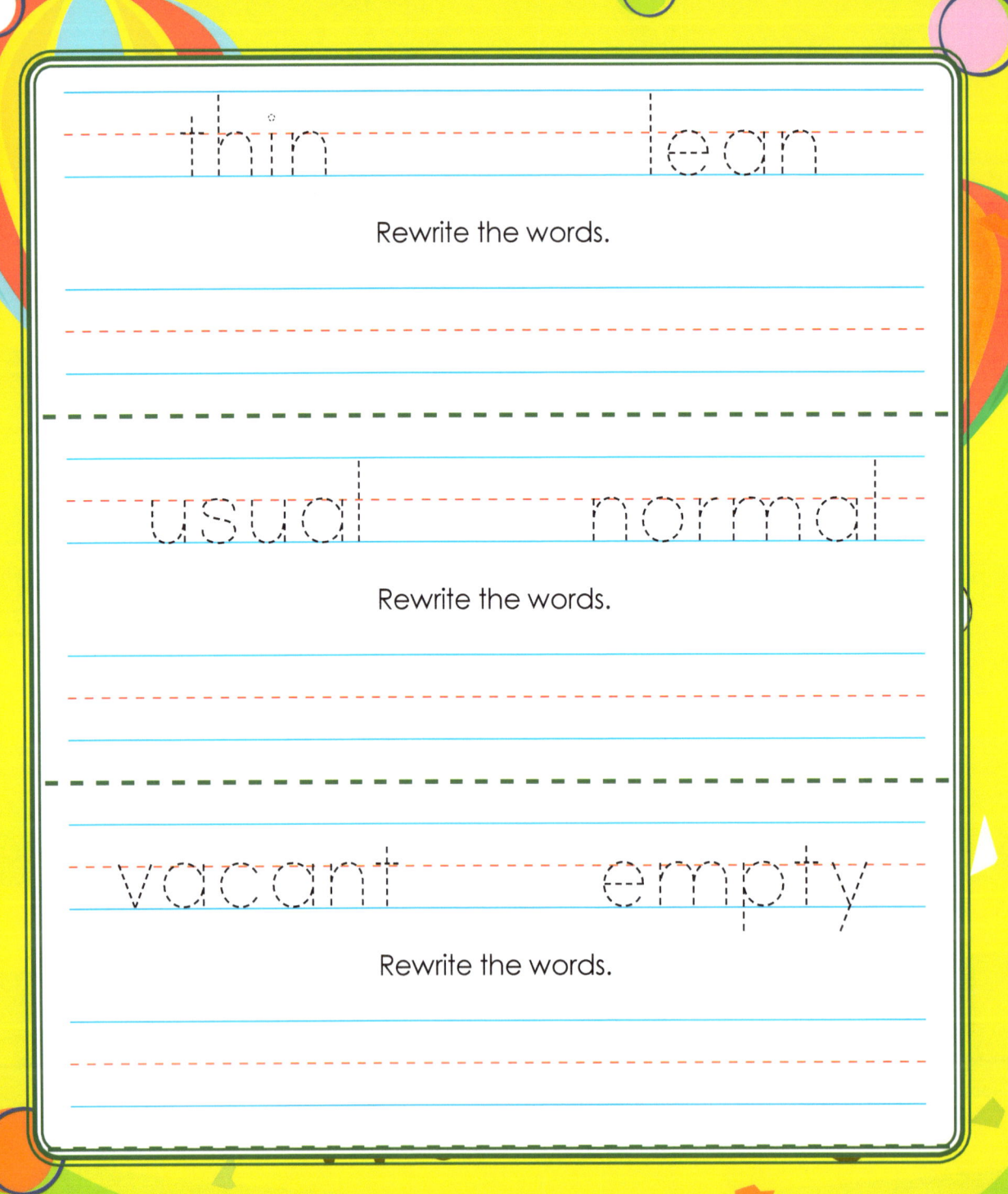

thin   lean

Rewrite the words.

usual   normal

Rewrite the words.

vacant   empty

Rewrite the words.

weak　　feeble

Rewrite the words.

above　　over

Rewrite the words.

stop　　cease

Rewrite the words.

exit　　　leave

Rewrite the words.

rest　　　relax

Rewrite the words.

strange　　　odd

Rewrite the words.

speak   talk

Rewrite the words.

sack   bag

Rewrite the words.

funny   silly

Rewrite the words.

present gift

Rewrite the words.

listen hear

Rewrite the words.

bunny rabbit

Rewrite the words.

garbage　　trash

Rewrite the words.

infant　　baby

Rewrite the words.

shut　　close

Rewrite the words.

rug   carpet

Rewrite the words.

shop   store

Rewrite the words.

hat   cap

Rewrite the words.

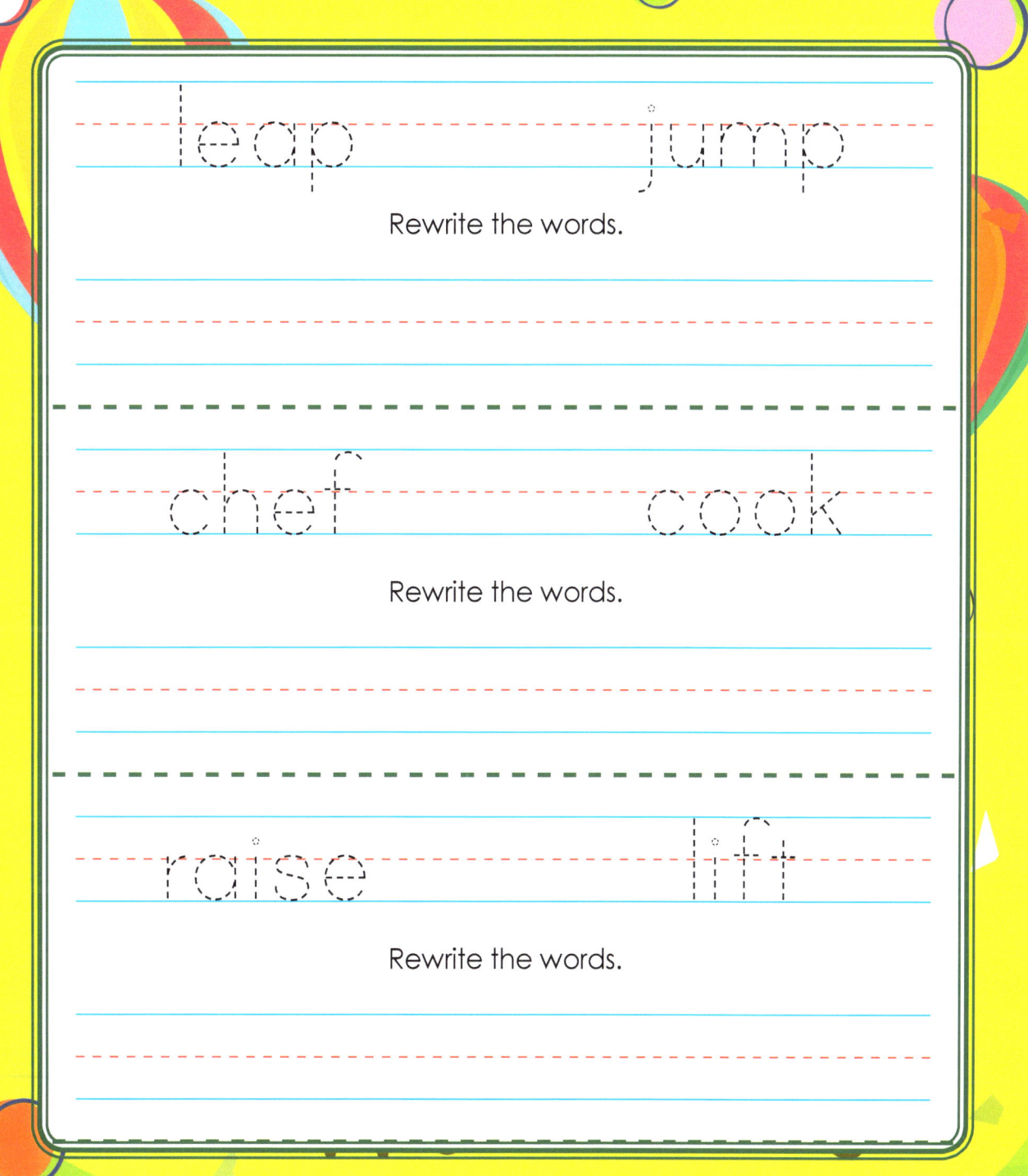

stone   rock

Rewrite the words.

near   close

Rewrite the words.

reply   answer

Rewrite the words.

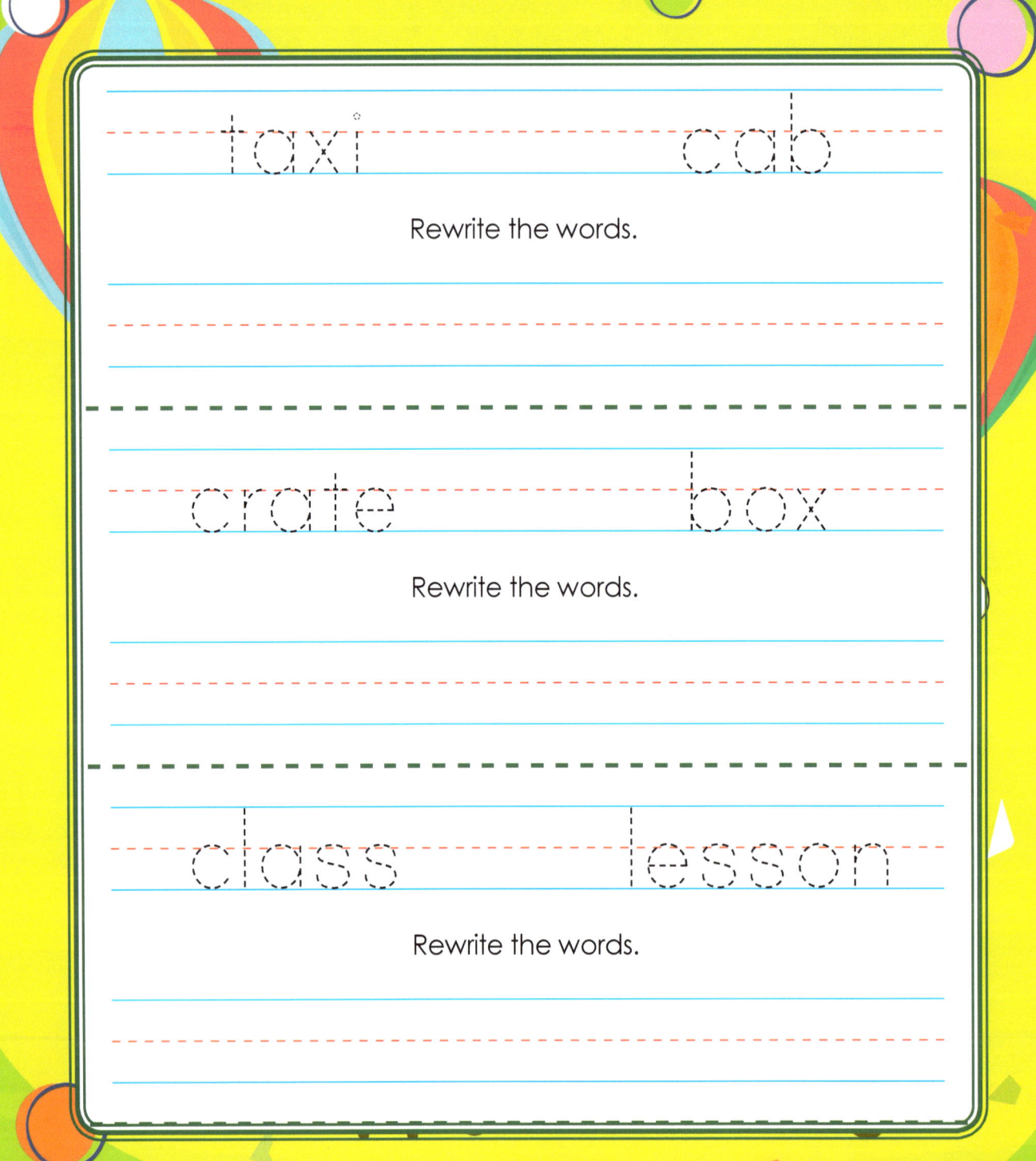

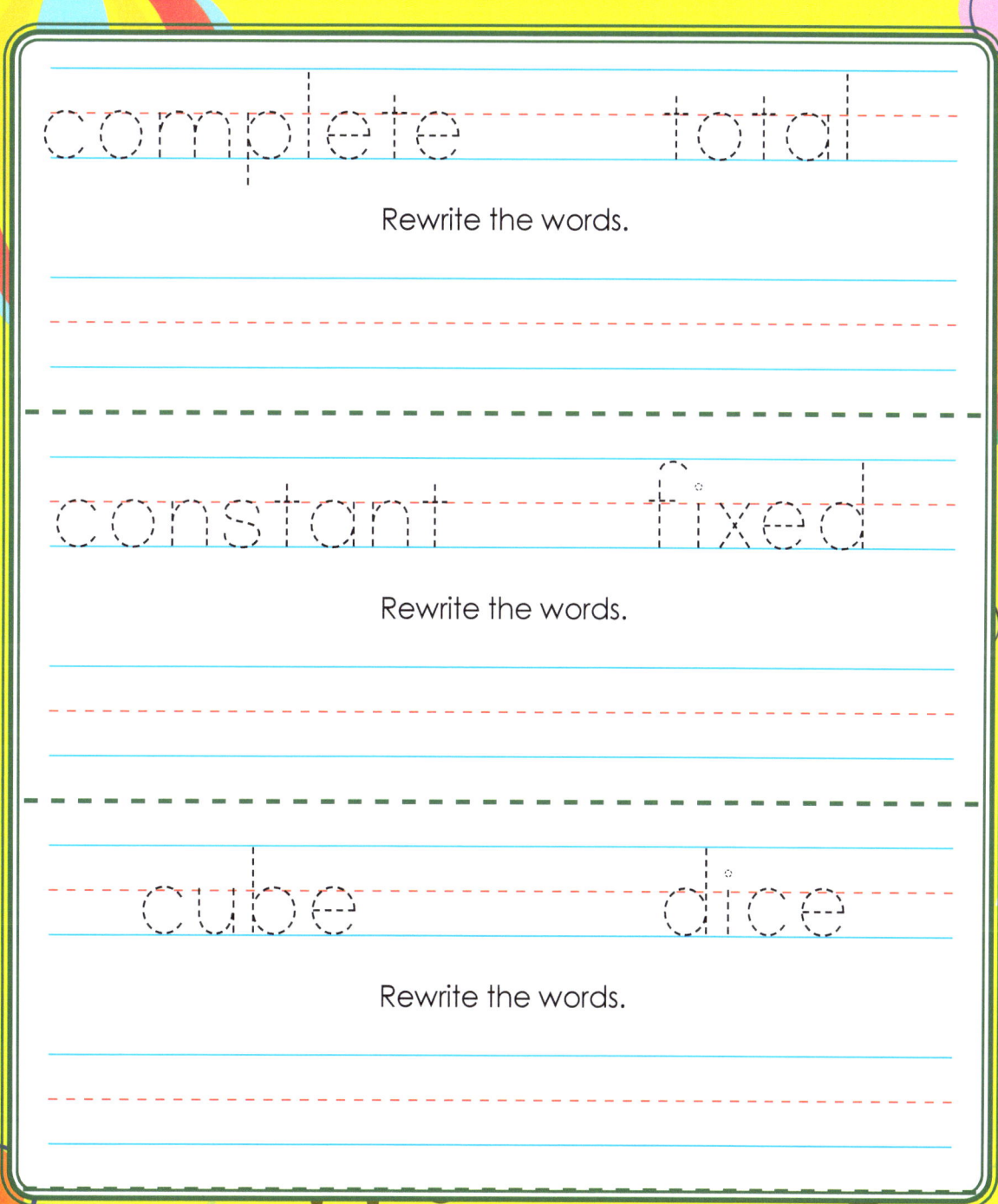

complete   total

Rewrite the words.

constant   fixed

Rewrite the words.

cube   dice

Rewrite the words.